BUILDING YOUR PEOPLE BUSINESS

Written & Illustrated

By

G.S.Gilmour

Dedication

To my God for bringing me my business,
and everything else.
To my Dad (Pop), who taught me people skills,
just by watching him.
To my awesome wife who is always positive.
To Don, Terry, Theron, Ron, Dave, Greg, Brad
and all of my business system mentors.

WHAT IS A PEOPLE BUSINESS ?

A PEOPLE BUSINESS is any business that involves
building networks of people for a common goal,
typically marketing products, services or ideas.
This book will help you navigate through building
a large networking business, while keeping a sense
of humor about it.
You will also learn how to KEEP THE PEOPLE in
your PEOPLE BUSINESS.
This book is about building others up,
while growing yourself and your business.

You Are Going To Be Great !
Let's have some fun.

REMEMBER
If you're not having fun, you're doing it wrong.

The fact is all businesses are people businesses. Until animals
or space aliens start buying your products you will be
in a people business.

CONTENTS

YOU'RE WEIRD

Before you get started building your PEOPLE BUSINESS, know one thing. You are different, maybe even weird. But that's OK ! You are daring to believe your life can be more than just a job with a boss. You are daring to believe there is more to life than a 9-5, rat-racing, bill-worrying, traffic-jamming, hanging-on-till-payday life. You know there has to be more … And You're Right !

You probably have done what you have been taught. Get a good education, get a good job and live happily ever after. How's that working out for you ? If you're reading this book, you probably are a person who wants more.

I remember in high school taking a test that was supposed to let you know what career you should pursue.(By the way, a career is just a long job) It had questions like "Do you like animals ? Do you like working with your hands ? Do you like working inside or outside ? Do you like people ?" A couple days later I got the results back. It said I should be a jazz-singing forest ranger. (I think that's what it said). The bottom line is nobody in high school knows what they want, except maybe a date.

Maybe you're like me, I was never a great student. I would always get a report card saying "capable of doing better" or "doesn't apply himself". I went to college but never got a degree. (but I ended up teaching at the University of Wisconsin. Figure that out) From high school on I did lots of different jobs until I started my People Business, which totally changed my life.

Here's a List of My Jobs

(This is to give you hope)

Fairgrounds maintenance, projectionist, diaper counter, caddy, pool installer, home construction, camera sales, picture framer, photography teacher, wedding photographer, musician, block layer, phone book delivery, fire hydrant painter, carpet layer, child care worker and house parent for emotionally disturbed children, guitar teacher, music store sales, gopher for millionaire, real estate salesman.

I was 38 years old when I started my People Business and retired with a high six figure income at the age of 40 in 1991. My wife and I have been free for 20 plus years.

Everyone wants the same thing ... More Time and More Money !
That's what YOU are daring to believe for.
Everyone wants to have more time and money, but now you are really doing something about it.

CONGRATULATIONS

Welcome to the Weirdo Club.
Welcome to the Road to Freedom.
It's never crowded and the view is awesome.

Note: You will be called weird by your friends and relatives until you are making a lot of money. Then you will be called Eccentric.

YOUR BROTHER-IN-LAW'S AN IDIOT

Not everyone will be excited about your new business. **DON'T PANIC !**

This is normal. I used to say "Make a list of your friends and relatives, then throw it away and start your business". But then my older, smarter brother got involved and built a huge People Business and also got free. I don't say that anymore. The people who are negative about your business are probably negative about everything. There are different reasons why someone may not be as excited as you are.

1. **THEY ARE NOT DREAMERS.** They can't see themselves doing what they "think" you are doing. They are content with their 9-5, two week vacation life. If you would call them a dreamer, they would be offended. You on the other hand would take that as a compliment.

2. **THEY KNEW SOMEONE** who may have done something similar or maybe even the same business and quit. So that means to them it doesn't work. How's that for logic ? I knew a guy who quit medical school. Does that mean medicine doesn't work ? When I got into my business, the only guy I ever knew that was involved in a networking business killed someone. I found out later that the percentage of murderes in our business was fairly low. Lower that the Post Office anyway.

When you talk to someone and they start the conversation with "I KNEW A GUY", Get Ready ! What I would do is ask them to tell me more about this person . Most of the time they won't even know their name. They just "heard of a guy".

One of my mentors, Don, kept hearing about a guy who lost his shirt in our business model. So finally he tracked the guy down. Come to find out he still had his shirt, wasn't negative about the business and was still involved. He just had some life challenges.

NOTE: I knew a guy who didn't build his People Business and HE DIED !

3. **THEY ARE JUST PLAIN SCARED** to do anything different from what they are doing even if what they are doing is not working for them. Many times it's just a low self image. They are afraid to get out of their comfort zone.

4. **THEY ARE FOCUSED ON SOMETHING ELSE**. They are not negative, it's just not the right timing now. It may be they're getting married, have a baby coming, a new job or are finishing college. Keep these people on your list, you may see them later.

5. RELATIVES AND FRIENDS can be your toughest critics. They think they know you. They watched all the dumb things you did growing up. They also know how to get to you. It might be a good idea to stay clear of the people who you know will be negative. At least until you're a little stronger in your business. I purposely did not show my "older, smarter brother" my business because I knew he would be negative. Because I kept building my business and was not worried about what my friends and family said or thought, both my brother and ex-boss got involved and built large businesses. My older, smarter brother and his wife got free in 1994. Hopefully you will have a positive supportive family and friends. If not you can send them postcards from Hawaii when you're free !

Walt Disney once said,
"THERE ARE THREE TYPES OF PEOPLE,
WELL POISONERS, LAWN MOWERS, AND LIFE ENHANCERS."

WELL POISONERS (Maybe your brother-in-law) These people are always looking at the negative. You know who they are, you're thinking about them right now. They always want to drag you down into their dark, glass half empty world. You will hear them say things like "What makes you think YOU can be wealthy ?" or "That thing won't work." Expect to encounter some well-poisoners on your journey.

LAWN MOWERS – This is where most people are mentally. They are just happy to live in their own small piece of the world. They take care of their own, but that's as far as it goes. These are nice people but they are not risk takers and are not business builders but are great customers.

LIFE ENHANCERS – These are the people who can change lives. People who can take their eyes off themselves and focus on others. They see a bigger, better world. These are the Big Dreamers, these are Your Business Builders.
THIS IS YOU …

Note: **A TRUE FRIEND** may not get involved in your business but will be supportive of your decision and will be excited for you, even if they don't understand what the heck you're doing or why you're doing it. If they are not supportive, they might not be a true friend.

Tip: Be careful who you listen to.

If someone attacks you for what you're doing, ask yourself, "Do I want this person's lifestyle ?" "Do they have the answer to my financial goals ?"" Will they help me ?" PROBABLY NOT ! They have nothing but negative to offer.

Keep away from well-poisoners. They will drain your energy.

WHY THE HECK AM I DOING THIS ?

It's very important, NO CRITICAL, to know why you're building your business. Know exactly what you want and what you're willing to do or to give up to get it.

Most people get involved for a small dream. A car payment, to pay off debt or to get a new boat. In my case I needed a house payment, that's all I wanted. We were in the process of losing our home, and that's back when it was hard to lose your home, now it's pretty easy. But once I got around other successful people and started listening to audios and watching videos, my vision and dreams got bigger and after I attended my first Major Business Seminar my dreams exploded. I started to see what my life could be. I was exposed to a lifestyle I didn't know existed. Two years later my wife and I walked away from our jobs.

If your WHY is not big enough or clear enough, you might not see much success. My WHY started out small, like most people, but got bigger as I built my business. FOCUS ON YOUR WHY. What do you really want from your business?

Next, what are you willing to do and how much time are you willing to devote to achieving your WHY ? Get a clear dollar amount in your head and on paper that will get you your WHY. Is it $100 a month ? $500, $5000, or maybe $50,000 a month ? As you build your People Business your WHY may grow and change. Take some time to figure out your REAL WHY.

Note: Napoleon Hill said " There is only one quality which one must possess to win, and that is **Definiteness of Purpose**, the knowledge of what one wants, and the burning desire to possess it."

MAKE SURE YOU'RE IN THE RIGHT BUSINESS

Now that we've figured out why you're building your business, let's make sure it's the right business. There are a few things to check and to watch for as you consider starting a networking business.

1. **Check with the Better Business Bureau** * www.bbb.org
   Don't just go to the internet. You will always find negative comments and opinions written by people who don't know what they're talking about.

2. **How long has the company been in business ?**
   If they talk about getting in on the ground floor. Watch Out ! The longer they have been in business, the better.

3. **Start Up Cost**
   If the Cost is substantial Be Careful. No money should be made by selling a starter kit.

4. **Buy-Back of Inventory ?**
   If you could be stuck with unsold inventory, Beware. Legitimate companies which require inventory purchases will usually "Buy Back" unsold products if you decide to quit the business.

5. **Do they require Sales to Customers ?**
   If Not, Stay Away !

6. **What is the Pay Structure ?**
   Does it make sense?

7. **Is There a Training System & People to Help You Build Your Business ?**

Some of the information on this page is from a pamphlet published by the Direct Selling Education Foundation, a Washington DC not-for-profit public education organization. It was prepared in cooperation with the Federal Trade Commission.

USE YOUR ~~JUNK, STUFF,~~ PRODUCTS

No business owner ever got wealthy buying from a competitor. This is the foundation of the success of any business, especially a networking business. Using your products or services is the biggest part of building your belief, and if you don't have belief in your products or services, you will not be able to talk to others about your business. IT WILL NOT WORK !

I remember asking my sponsor when I first started my business, "What's the difference between Tide laundry detergent and the stuff we have ?" He just looked at me and said, "About $60,000 a year". Then I said "What if I don't like our toothpaste ?" Once again, he just looked me in the eye and said very slowly. "LIKE THE TOOTHPASTE". I finally got it ! Personal use is just part of playing the game. If you want the money, you have to play the game.

A couple of weeks into my new business I listened to an audio called "TURN UP THE VOLUME". After hearing it, I went through the house and threw away anything that I could buy from my own store. I did this when my wife, who was not yet on board with my new business, was not at home. The problem was we were broke and couldn't replace the products right away. So we did without for awhile. I refused to buy a competitor's product. When she saw that I had thrown away all of our stuff, she thought I'd lost it. Then I said to her, "You have two weeks to change your cosmetics to My Company." People always tell me, "I'd never do that". And I always say, " That's why I'm free and You're Not". I was serious about my business. I bought the ranch, burnt my bridges and until YOU do that you won't make the Big Money.

Personal Use is a big part of your business. Your group will do what you do.
Would you want people to duplicate you ?

15

TAKE THE STUPID TEST

NOTE: Personal use builds your belief in your products and your business. Why would anyone want to buy your products if you're not using them. You can't teach something you're not doing.

PLEASE don't play around with this. I watched business owners fail from not being loyal to their own company.

Tip: You will get a lot of customers from people seeing you use your products. Always keep samples handy. (Junk in the Trunk)

Tip: Your group will do half of what you do.

BE LOYAL TO YOUR BUSINESS

PLAY BY THE RULES

In any business or game there are rules to follow to be successful or win the game. Your business is no different.

For example; when I was in the real estate business there were certain things I had to do to be successful. I had to get home listings, make cold calls, do open houses and many other things. It didn't matter whether I liked to do those things or not. If I wanted to make the money, I needed to play the game. There is a high turnover rate in real estate because people are not willing to do what it takes. Could they be successful ? Yes, if they played by the rules.

When I first got involved in my People Business, I had known people who had "tried" the same or similar businesses and quit. So I did something most people never do. I asked someone who was making a lot of money in his People Business,

"What did you do that these other people did not do ?"
And he told me. Here's what he said:

1. Successful people **consistently** expose their business or products to others. In our networking organization, he said. "Less than 5% of the people present their business plan 3 or more times a week." If you have a good work ethic and are willing to share your business, it's easy to become a superstar in your group. You don't have to do it good, just do it !

2. The people who make the money always use their own products or services. 100% PERSONAL USE.

3. Successful people connect with someone who is already successful in their business model; a person who has a stake in their success. They have a coach/mentor. If you're going to walk through a mine field, walk in the steps of a person who has already made it through.

4. Successful people listen and are teachable. This is sometimes tricky. A person who builds a large networking business needs to be tough and confident, yet be able to submit their ego to a coach/mentor.

5. People who build big businesses are always improving themselves. They plug into their teaching system; **seminars**, **books**, **audios**. Successful people never stop growing. If you think you already know it all, you've already started your slide backwards.

6. Successful people take ownership of their business.

If you ask people who have quit/failed in your particular business, "Did you do at least these six things ?" The answer, I can guarantee, will be NO ! Here's the kind of thing they will say. "I can't believe they wanted me to go to their meetings and listen to their audios." "I don't need that Rah Rah stuff." I was one of those guys when I first got in. I didn't want to go to meetings. The person who got me involved said I needed to go to a large meeting in Boulder, Colorado. Guess what I said, "I don't need that Rah Rah stuff," plus I was broke. Then he challenged my manhood. He said; "I thought you were serious." That made me mad, so I decided to go just to show him that I was serious. I still couldn't afford it, but I made a QUALITY DECISION to do everything I could to get there. (17 hour car ride) That was a great lesson for me. Once I made the decision to get something done, miracles happened.

I decided to sell some of my things. (Note: I wasn't smart enough to sell products from my business.) I sold my video camera, a keyboard, I even sold some of my older, smarter brother's stuff that I borrowed and forgot to return. Don't tell him. (I hope I'm giving you hope that anybody can get free)

I did whatever I could to get to Boulder. I still didn't have enough money to make the trip and was running out of time. But then the miracle happened. I got a check out of the blue that I was not expecting. It was just enough to get me there. That seminar made all the difference in my belief and changed my life. Oh, by the way, I took one guy with me, the only person in my business at the time, my friend "Bart". That business now is huge. If I wouldn't have listened to my coach, I know I would probably be one of those guys who would say, "I tried that thing, it doesn't work."

Every Business or Network has certain activities you need to do to be successful. Make a QUALITY DECISION to

PLAY BY THE RULES

Note: Your Business Mentors have given you the quickest way to be successful. Don't shortcut the shortcut.

YOU ARE NOT SCUM ... BUILDING YOU

GOD CREATED YOU FOR GREATNESS. YOU ARE NOT MEANT TO BE AVERAGE.

Everyone starts their business at different levels of self-confidence, belief and skills. These all can change and improve. People tell me all the time, "I'm just a shy person," or "I'm not good at meeting people", and " I don't like talking to strangers," or "I just don't see myself being wealthy." Remember, YOUR PERSONALITY WAS BUILT, NOT GIVEN. The key to making changes is your Dream or Vision. It has to be big enough and real enough to make you want to change.

HOW DO I CHANGE ?

People who change their lives for the better always have a vision or a hope of what their life could be. That's why they go to college. They have a vision of what their life will be if they get a degree. They spend tons of money and time and most get into major debt to get a piece of paper.

Decide what your future looks like and go for it. Quit looking at your past, it's past. Start looking forward. My friend Theron always says, "Every time I look back I get tired." Keep looking and moving forward. Keep your Dreams in front of you.

IF NOTHING CHANGES, NOTHING CHANGES

If you don't change what you're doing and thinking, you will get what you got. How's that working for you ? Nobody likes change but if you keep your eyes on the prize, it's much easier to make the changes that will bring your dreams to life.

LET'S GET STARTED

Don't try to change everything at once. Do a little at a time. If you want to change anything in your life, take small steps. If you try to do too much you can get discouraged. You can do this ! One step at a time.

CHANGE YOUR THINKING, REBOOT YOUR BRAIN

You must change your thoughts about who you are. Everyone has a picture of who they are because of past experiences in life: how you were raised, how your parents or teachers talked to you and treated you. (Maybe words like stupid, lazy or shy may have been used.) None of these are true unless you want them to be. The only way to change how you think, which will change how you act, is to: **READ, LISTEN, SPEAK, DREAM**.

READ: Positive attitude books, flush out the negative. If you don't like to read, use audio books. I am a lousy reader, so I learned better by listening than by reading. Do what works for you. The main thing is that you start reprogramming your brain with positive thoughts.

LISTEN: to your mentors that will encourage, uplift and believe in you. Fill your mind with positive audios about your business. Listen to people's stories of success. Don't listen to critics. Start thinking about what YOUR SUCCESS STORY will be. It's going to be a great story !

SPEAK: positive affirmations about who you want to be and what your goals are. Speak in the present tense. Example: "I am great with people, I love to meet new people, I am making $100,000 plus a year in my business."

Tip: Do this in the bathroom or your car. People already think you're goofy, don't give them more ammunition.

Your subconscious does not know the difference between a lie and the truth. It takes it all in and believes it. Most people have been bombarding their subconscious with negative thoughts (Lies) about who they are and what they deserve in life. Change that right now. SPEAK ONLY POSITIVE.

Speak positive about your business and your business associates in front of them and behind closed doors. Don't derail your business with negative talk. Find good things to say about your group and your business.

Don't Puke On Your Group !

DREAM: Develop your dream. If it's strong enough, it will move everything else forward. Write down your dream and have it where you can see it all the time. Write It and Speak It ! Your words have power. Make sure your dream really moves you and gets you excited. If it doesn't get you excited and move you to action, it's not your real dream. Get a BIG DREAM and protect it. Never let it go.

DREAMS & VISIONS
YOUR VISION FUELS YOUR DREAMS
Dreams like Homes, Cars, Boats, Travel, and Giving to Charities
all come true if your vision is a successful Money Making Business.
YOUR VISION PAYS FOR YOUR DREAMS

Tip: Share your dreams with your mentors so they can direct you on the right path. Don't share your dreams with dream-stealers. You know who they are.
"Don't cast your pearls before swine"

READ * LISTEN * SPEAK * DREAM
These all work together to reprogram your thinking,
Which will change your world.

HELPFUL BOOK LIST
Self Confidence & Belief

You Can If You Think You Can * Norman Vincent Peale

Created To Win * Kevin Baerg

Confidence & Power In Dealing With People * Les Goblin

How To Win Friends & Influence People * Dale Carnegie

Enthusiasm Makes The Difference * Norman Vincent Peale

The Go-Getter * Peter B. Kyne

Life Is Tremendous * Charlie Jones

Magic Of Believing * Claude M. Bristol

Magic Of Thinking Big * David J. Schwartz

Greatest Salesman * Og Mandino

The Tongue - A Creative Force * Charles Capps

Think And Grow Rich * Napoleon Hill

University Of Success * Og Mandino

WHO AND WHERE ARE THEY ?

This chapter is about Prospecting. Finding people who want or need your products, services or business. We will break it down into two sections. Prospecting for Customers/Clients and Prospecting for Business Builders.

THE CUSTOMER/CLIENT HUNT

Hopefully your networking group has sales training for your particular products or services. This section is about WHO to talk to, WHERE to find them and HOW to help potential clients. Remember, if you're not using the products you're presenting to your clients, forget about being successful. It's just not going to happen.

WHO AM I LOOKING FOR ? Well let's start with Family, Friends and Co-workers. They will be your highest percentage in the beginning and probably the most loyal.

"How do I approach family, friends, co-workers ?" "What do I say ?"
Let's start with what NOT to say. Here are some general tips to help you out.

1. **DON'T BE A SALESMAN**. See yourself as an advisor helping to solve a problem they might have. Let's say your products are vitamins. Talk about how excited you are, finally, to have some energy to get through the day. Talk about how you felt before and after you started using your product. Tell your story without techno-babble or sales jargon. Just speak plain english. Stay away from company names. As soon as people hear a company name they are expecting a sales pitch. Listen for ways you can help them solve their problems. Always remember you are an Advisor, not a Salesperson.

2. **LET GO OF NON-BUYERS**. Usually only a small percentage of people will be buyers. Some Will, Some Won't, So What ! Move on. If they're not interested, wish them well and keep moving. But, you say " They really need my product", it doesn't matter, move on.

Everybody has two lists. A VENT LIST and a CHANGE LIST. You hear people at work complaining about all sorts of things. "I wish I could lose weight", "I really need to get in shape", "I hate my job." But very few people are willing to do anything about it. They are just VENTING. Even if you have the answer to their problem with your product, they still won't buy. Just understand that so you don't get frustrated. It's not you, it's them. Then there's the Change List. Certain people WILL change the things they need to change. The problem is we don't know who they are, they look just like the Venters. We only know who they really are when we offer them the solution to their problem.

3. **LISTEN**. Let people talk so you can understand how to help them. Take interest in them. Talk TO them, not AT them. Make a friend.
4. **NO HYPE OR OUTRAGEOUS CLAIMS ABOUT YOUR PRODUCT.** Just tell them what the product did for you. Don't sound like an infomercial. Be a real person.
5. **GET REFERRALS**. Magic words, "Do You Know Anybody Who?" Let's say you have weight-loss products. You could say "Who do you know who's looking to get in better shape?" Never ask that person if they want to lose weight. I hope you get that. The "Boy you're really fat" approach doesn't work all that well.

6. **SAMPLES,SAMPLES,SAMPLES.** Always have "Junk in the Trunk". Be ready at all times to give samples of your product. It's the best way to get your product business started.

Let's say you have meal replacement bars in your business. It's easy to say to someone, "Have you ever tried meal replacement bars? Here, try this one and let me know what you think." One couple in my business gives people a basket with a bunch of different product samples. They give the people 10 days to try everything and they tell them, "You can buy or not buy, we just want you to try them." There is no pressure to buy. They have never used that approach without getting at least one sale. Some groups call this Drop & Shop. Invest in your business. Invest in Samples.

Let's get back to talking to friends, relatives and co-workers. One great way to present your products to this group is **CAUSE MARKETING.** People love to help people out. It makes them feel good, especially if you're a friend or relative. Here's how it works. Let's say you are a single mom with two small children. Let the prospect know why you're building your business. " I'm trying to make some extra money for my kid's college fund" or " I want to send my children to a private school." If you're building your business, you have a reason why you're doing it. Let them know why. Let them help you.

You should be excited about your products or service. Just find other people to get excited with you.

Let's recap: **DON'T BE A SALESMAN, BE AN ADVISOR * LET GO OF NON-BUYERS * LISTEN TO YOUR PROSPECTS * NO HYPE * SPEAK REAL GET REFERRALS * GIVE SAMPLES * USE CAUSE MARKETING HAVE FUN !**

Don't sell the product, sell the results. Talk about the person they will become by using your product. Figure out the best way for you to build your product business. It's your business, be creative.

It's important to connect with a mentor. They can help you with your product marketing techniques. Learn everything you can about your products but don't get too technical. Keep it light.

HUNT FOR THE ELUSIVE BUSINESS BUILDER

The reality is we never know who's going to build a big business. We just look for people we can work with and help. We look for people who are looking for more and are willing to do something about it. YOU ARE THAT PERSON !

BUILDING YOUR LIST

If you're married, start with your wedding guest list. Think about who you went to school with or co-workers, neighbors and teachers past and present. Your dentist, doctor, pet groomer, landscaper could all be good prospects. Just start writing down names, one name will remind you of other names.

Here are some more ideas:

Friends, parents, grandparents, sisters, brothers, cousins, uncles, aunts, church members, mailman, minister, florist, attorney, insurance agent, accountant, pharmacist, veterinarian, optometrist, real estate salesperson, nurse, student, security guard, fireman, music teacher.

College and high school year books are also great sources for names. The most successful person in your business could be the person you meet tomorrow. Be ready !

Always try to have a long prospect list. This will keep you from getting and sounding desperate. Don't prejudge, just make your list. Don't forget to ask your friends and family or anybody, "Who do you know who's looking for more ?" I'm always surprised who builds the business and who doesn't. It's not our job to figure it out. It's our job to expose our business and give people hope.

YOU MAY NEVER NEED TO PROSPECT STRANGERS

Everybody knows about 150 people. Those people know about 150 people. Get where I'm going ? Just play the "Who do you know ?" game. If you ask everybody YOU know who THEY know, it adds up quickly. Let's say you ask just 5-10 people, "Who do you know who is looking for more money or more time ?" You will probably get 5-7 more names and that's the beginning of a HUGE BUSINESS !

WHO DO THEY KNOW ?

WE ALL KNOW A BUNCH OF PEOPLE, ASK US !

WHERE ARE THEY ?

When a new person starts their business, they always ask, "Where do I meet people ?" The answer is you meet them where they are. There are billions of people out there and you're only looking for a few. The odds are in your favor !

If you are always ready and "In the mode" (the prospecting mode) you may never need to go out looking for or (Spearing) prospects. Just live your life and you will run into people. The new person always goes "mall-crawling" in the beginning to meet new people but that usually doesn't work out. You may meet a mall guard as they are throwing you out.

You need to develop your own style. Don't be afraid to fail. I will give you some techniques that worked for others but they might not work for you. Figure it out.

Here are some ideas of places to make new friends: I always liked hotels and here's why. You can ask anybody in a hotel, "Where you from?" It's never weird in a hotel. It's a great ice-breaker. Another way to meet people in a hotel is to ask at the front desk about renting meeting rooms. As your business grows you may need one. You can meet three or four people from the hotel staff just by doing that; the desk clerk, manager and maybe catering person.

Here are more ideas where to meet people: sporting events, coffee shops, school events, clubs, classes, fitness centers, or weddings. One person I know met most of his people at gas stations. Whatever works.

Open houses can be a great place to dream build and meet people. I also liked going to small retail shops where someone would wait on me. There are probably a bunch of those in your town.

I never liked going out and just wandering. I liked to have a project in my head before I went out. I would think, "I'm going to learn everything I can about HD TVs or carpets, kayaks or maybe furniture" and guess what ? I WOULD MEET PEOPLE !

Go to places where there are things you are interested in: sporting good stores, golf shops, fabric stores, hobby shops or maybe car dealerships. What ever gets you excited or builds a dream while you meet new friends.

GET LOST

Here's a way to meet 5-10 people in a few hours. My friend Darrell taught me the technique of "GETTING LOST". Here's how it works: He would go up to anyone and ask, "Are you from around here?" If they were, he would ask directions to a men's clothing store or maybe an office supply store or coffee shop. If they weren't from around there, he would ask where they were from. Either way a great way to start a conversation. He then would chit-chat a bit, ask questions and make a friend. He always introduced himself and they always gave him their names. With this technique he could talk to anyone. He didn't have to wait for an opening, he was in control. But here's the real magic, he then would go to whatever place he asked directions about and do the same thing. He felt it was dishonest if he didn't go to the place he asked about. I love that. If you want lots of names fast, GET LOST !

QUIT THINKING

Here are a few basics to remember: Be Positive, Smile, Be Friendly, Make Someone's Day with Uplifting Words, Listen to People and Let Them Talk. Don't worry about what they think. Just be yourself and make a friend.

Too many people worry too much about what strangers think about them. The fact is they don't think about you at all. They are thinking about themselves.

PROSPECT

I was one of those people who would make excuses why I shouldn't talk to a certain prospect. "They look too busy, they're probably not looking, what if they yell at me ?" All kinds of things would go through my head. Many times I would not talk to someone because of what I thought they might think. Dumb ! Then I got mad. I would say to myself, "I'm not going to let this person dictate my future, they are not going to stop me from building my business". I got myself all worked up. The problem with that is when I finally talked to the person, I was mad. Then I learned something from my friend and mentor Terry. He said "You can't think two thoughts at once. Replace the negative thoughts with

"DO IT NOW, DO IT NOW, DO IT NOW !"

It works, try it. Here's a little tip: Say it to yourself, not out loud or they might think you're weird and walk away. Don't ask me how I know this.

BREAKING THE ICE

The best approach is the one you use ! Nothing works all the time. The most important thing is you feel comfortable using it. There is no magic approach. YOU ARE THE MAGIC. You turn strangers into friends. An ice breaker is anything that starts a conversation: weather, sports, kids, asking directions, complimenting someone or just a simple "Hi". The key is to be sincere and natural. A smile will always be helpful.

Think of icebreakers, or prospecting in general, as fishing. All you are doing is casting your line and waiting for a bite. Most people never wet their line and wonder why they are not successful. 1. Go where the fish are. They are not on your couch. 2. Use the right bait. 3. The fish have to be hungry. 4. Be patient. Don't expect every fish to bite. More casts equals more fish. Go wet your line.

ICEBREAKER EXAMPLES

Here are a few ideas for icebreakers. It's important that you feel comfortable using them. You don't want them to sound like a script, even if they are.

OUT AND ABOUT
Are you from around here ? Do I look familiar to you ?
Can you tell me how to get to ___ ?
Did you used to work at ___ ?
Did you used to work with my wife/husband ?
Are there any good restaurants around here ?
Where's a good place to get a ___ ?

STANDING IN LINES
At a grocery store- Is that ___ any good ?
Have you tried the ___ ? My kids love that ___
Other lines- Don't you love standing in lines ?
Do you believe this weather ?
Are you ready for spring/summer/fall/winter ?

MAKE SOMEONE'S DAY
(Look for something to comment on)
That's a great tie/ shirt/blouse. Where did you get it ?
I love your ___ . Is it hard to find those ?
That's a great mustache/beard.
That's a great laptop/purse/etc. Where did you get it ?

CURRENT EVENTS - LAST NIGHT'S TV
(Keep it positive)
Did you see the game last night ? Have you seen___ ?
What do you think about ___ ?

MORE ICE BREAKERS

AT THE GAS STATION
How's the gas mileage with that car ?
What a great looking car. What year is that ?
How about these prices ?
I was looking to get one of those. How's it handle ?

GENERAL GREETINGS
How's your day going ? You having a great day ?
You look like you're having a great day.
For people working in stores- Having fun yet ? Then smile.
I also like to tell people they are doing a great job.
These are just suggestions. Work on your own.

Remember you are just fishing to see who will bite. Some people won't even acknowledge you. Just smile, it's all part of the game. When you're out there, always remind yourself of the prize. You're doing things that others won't do, so you will live a life others won't live.

Someone out there is waiting for someone like you to change their life forever. What right do you have to withhold a great business that could change their lives ? Get your eyes off yourself and on the other person.

Tip: Make your greeting a little "different" to make them think. You are trying to get a direct response. Not just a "What's Sup ?"

F.O.R.M.

WE STARTED A CONVERSATION, NOW WHAT ?

People may get good at icebreakers but don't know what to do
after they have made a connection and how to transition to business.
Let's start with "What should I talk about ?"
Use F.O.R.M. This stands for:

FAMILY * OCCUPATION * RECREATION * MESSAGE

The idea is to ask people about themselves; ask questions, then shut up. Let them talk, don't interrupt. My friend Theron always said, "Never miss the chance to say nothing." Great advice ! You have been with people who never let you finish your sentence before they interrupt. What they are saying is "What I have to say is more important than what you have to say." Don't be that guy ! Notice I didn't say, "Don't be that girl." That's because girls would never interrupt, right ?

DON'T MAKE MEETING PEOPLE A BIG DEAL

Just go out and make somebody feel good ! Be a positive light in a negative world. Start out small if you have to. Just say "Hi". Get out there and make somebody smile. You are excited about your business so go share that excitement. My business totally changed my life and my family's life. What if the person who contacted me would have been afraid to talk to me or written me off as a bad prospect ? People are waiting for you. Don't disappoint them. They need what you have to give. GO SHARE THE DREAM !

I'M JUST THERE TO MAKE A FRIEND
Exposing Your Business Model

The success or failure of any networking business all comes down to showing your business model to a new person. It's all about numbers. How many people did you talk to about your products or your business plan ? "He who shows the most plans wins." Although the percentage of people who get involved in your business will dramatically increase if you learn not to be a jerk.

My good friend and mentor Theron would say, "When I show the business plan, I'm just there to make a friend. I just show the plan to kill time." His sponsoring percentage was very high because he treated people right. That's what it's all about. Treating people like you want to be treated, keeping things simple and making a friend.

Your job is to SHOW people your business not get them in. Don't worry about who gets involved and who doesn't. That's not your job. Getting involved is their job. Remember, "It's not your performance, it's the quality of the audience." Some Will, Some Won't, So What. NEXT ! I tell people "Your NEXT PLAN is the most important one !"

Studies have been done on why people get involved or why they do not. It seems the business plan is not as important as how they feel about the person showing them the plan. Here's the two things that are most important to the prospect; CAN I TRUST THIS PERSON AND WILL THEY HELP ME ? Sounds simple, but that's it. If the person is not looking, it doesn't matter how wonderful you are, they ain't gettin' in. Timing is another factor. They just don't have the time right now.

Now let's talk about some other things you can do to increase your sponsoring percentage.

SMILE, sounds simple but it's a big deal. Watch your posture, you should be relaxed. If you're relaxed, your prospect will be relaxed. If I was showing my business model at a coffee shop or restaurant, I would always lean back in the chair or booth. Give them space. Don't get in their face or space.

My father taught me to talk to people like you are already old friends. You talk differently to old friends, more relaxed. I always had to watch how loud I was talking. I would get excited about showing my business and my volume would get louder. The good news about that is people three tables over would ask me about my business. I was showing a guy my business in a coffee shop when he stopped me and said "I've already seen this twice." "By who ?" I said. "You" It was a small coffee shop and he had heard me talk to other people. Try not to get too excited or too loud.

It's important to get to know the prospect a little. I would chit-chat for fifteen to twenty minutes before I showed the business plan. I would ask questions about their job, their family and how they spent their off-time. I was listening for a hot button, something they were looking for. Ron, a mentor of mine, always said, "You're looking for a WANT, a NEED or a DESIRE when you're talking to a prospect about your business." If you find their hot button, gear the whole plan on how they can get it.

People sometimes qualify the prospect before they show them their business. Example: Do you see yourself making __ dollars doing what you're doing in the next 2 years ? Is that of interest ? Would you have 5-10 hours to put into that if I could show you how to get it ?

What you give people after the plan to take home can and will make the difference. If the person who showed me would not have given me an audio, I would not have gotten involved.

One more thing, BUSINESS POSTURE. Remember they need you, you don't need them. You just need to show enough people your business to find the right folks. THEY ARE OUT THERE !

Tip: You're just there to make a friend.
They want to know "Can I trust you and will you help me ?"
Find a WANT,NEED or DESIRE

KILLING YOUR TV

Get rid of your distractions. If you're serious about building a large business it will take a time commitment. I know you're busy. Busy people get things done. You may have to give up a few things short term, maybe a little less TV time. Perhaps the softball team could make it without you for a season or you could cut back on your golfing. Remember this is short term. It's called **Delayed Gratification**. Giving up something now to get something much better later. My older, smarter brother gave up golf until he achieved a certain level in his business. Now he golfs whenever and wherever he wants. He recently went to Ireland for a month just to golf. (He might've also hit a pub or two) Give up a little now for a lot later.

Another place where people spend a lot of their time is kid's activities. Parents feel if they don't attend every kid event, every baseball and soccer game, tennis match and Pom-Pom practice, they are lousy parents. Try asking your kids, "Would you mind if I miss a few of your events so we can go to Disney World every year or maybe tour all the major league ballparks in the country or take your whole Pom-Pom squad to a theme park ?" "What do you think ?" My father was always going to meetings in the evenings when I played baseball. I knew he could not make all the games. It made it extra special when he did get to a game. You don't need to be at everything.

I asked my good friend Norm, who has built a huge People Business, how he dealt with missing some of his kids' events as he was building his business. He said "I always put the good of the whole family above an individual." In his case the good of the family was building their business and getting financially free. His kids have an unbelievable lifestyle because of his decision.

Trust me, your kids will thank you when you take them to Hawaii for a few weeks or go on an African Safari or go to Paris for a month to learn French. How about paying for your daughter's ridiculously expensive wedding ? You are not a bad parent for missing a few events. Put your family's good above the individual. Great advice. The Bible says, " A good man leaves an inheritance for his children's children." It says nothing about not missing a T-Ball game or Pom-Pom practice.

Successful people figure out their time leaks. TIME MANAGEMENT, if you will. Every time I heard someone talk about time management I cringed, sounds like school homework to me. I was never big on homework but engineer types love that sort of thing. I am not an engineer type but I did have to figure out my way of getting the job done and stay on task. You will also have to figure out which things are important and which things are not.

The best way to stay consistent with your valuable time is, of course, setting business hours. (I will talk a lot about business hours) Your job has business hours, so why not your business ? One of the biggest mistakes I see people make is trying to take their left-over time to build their business. Most of the time, there is no left-over time. It never works. You must make time for your business just like you make time for your job. My friend Paul said, " For every hour I put in my job, I will put that many hours in my business." He was free in less than 2 years, and has been free for over twenty years.

You may have to make some hard choices building your business. You must decide what is most important to your future and your family's future. Relative events can also be a big distraction. Example: You may have to choose missing Aunt Tilly's third wedding to go to a business meeting. Your relatives will not understand. Remember this is short term. You will probably be able to make Aunt Tilly's fourth wedding.

Tip: Practice Delayed Gratification
Put the Family's Good Above the Individual
Set Business Hours

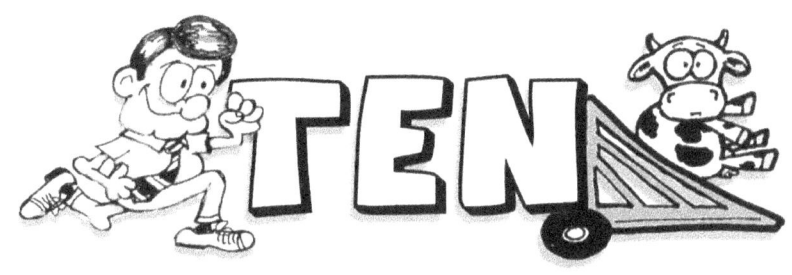

FAST MOVING TRAIN

I heard an audio one time that said, " Your business is a fast moving train. Slow people don't catch fast moving trains and people don't jump off fast moving trains." Momentum is a key factor if you're going to build a large successful networking business.

I was told once , "Slow and steady wins the race." That would be true if you were hoeing a row of beans. But if you're building a People Business, slow and steady only keeps you in the game. If you want to win the game and make the big money you need to go hard and fast. Remember we are looking for momentum not perfection. I tell people I'm working with to just "GO BOZO!" "Don't worry about screwing up, you will." " DO SOMETHING AND SOMETHING HAPPENS."

Just like a train, your business can start out slow and then start picking up speed. The key is once you're up to speed, DON'T STOP, KEEP MOVING ! As soon as you stop or slow down people will jump off your business train. You are the engine that moves your business forward. Keep it moving fast. Keep active. Keep your business hours full.

Early in my business I hosted a very successful multi-millionaire networking person. I was dropping him off at the airport when suddenly he turned to me, stuck his finger in my chest and said, "If I could tell you one thing, MOMENTUM !" I always remembered that and he was so right. You are a fast moving train. Run it hard and fast.

Tip: Don't start and stop with building your business.
Keep activity consistently high

WAIT FOR ME, I'M YOUR LEADER

John Quincy Adams said, "If your actions inspire others to dream more, learn more, do more and become more, You Are A Leader."

You can't create a leader but you might be able to grow one. Developing leaders in your organization is all about giving people space to make mistakes and find their own paths. Encouragement and believing in someone can be magical. You might be the only person in their life to say, "You can do it, I believe in you." Some people grew up with parents who never praised them. I'm amazed to hear the stories from people about how they were raised with nothing but criticism and negative reinforcement. A leader should be the one who lifts people up and believes in them.

There is no such thing as "Constructive Criticism". It's always destructive. Always focus on what people are doing right. They should always feel better after talking to you. My father was the master of this. He was a city manager for a small town in Michigan. He had to deal with all sorts of people and problems. I watched him do what I call a "Pop Sandwich." (I call my dad Pop) Here's how it works; If someone made a mistake or was not doing what they were supposed to do, he would always start out by praising the person for something they had done. Then he would address the problem. He would ask the person what they think we should do about the problem. He would involve them in the solution. Then he would praise or thank them for the great work. He was always raising people up. So praise, talk about the problem and involve them in the solution, then praise or thank them. A POP SANDWICH.

Tip: Don't Criticize or Condemn, Lift People Up
Believe in People * Use the Pop Sandwich

IF YOU'RE NOT MOVING FORWARD,
YOU'RE NOT THE LEADER

Leaders lead. Your group needs to see you moving forward. They are watching you. They need to see you ACTIVE. Remember, you are the engine that moves your business forward. Most people need to see many people succeed in their networking business before they believe they can do it. A leader just needs to see one person succeed or just to know it's possible.

WORKING WITH YOUR PEOPLE

Always keep in mind this might be the first time your new person is in their own business. It can take a little time for them to get a "business attitude". They are coming from the job world where someone else was making all the decisions for them. Most people you will deal with will have an employee mentality. Help them start thinking like a business person. Remind them, they are the boss now.

Help your group to develop positive business habits. Most people are where they are in life because of their habits, good or bad. You don't need to or shouldn't point out their bad habits. They know what they are. When I deal with someone, I always say, "Here's what the successful people do." Always stay on the positive not the negative. They probably already have a boss at their job, they don't need another one. They need a mentor and a friend.

Anytime you need to let someone know what they need to do, always bring them back to WHY they started their business. Remind them of their wants, needs or desires. Keep the dream alive !

You should always be looking downline in your business for people you can develop a long-term relationship with. Most of your leaders will be found in depth. Your business stability will depend on how well you can build depth in your business.

Never put pressure on anyone. If they feel pushed, you could push them right out of the business. Work with their goals, not yours. Work with their time schedule, not yours.

To find out how to help someone without putting pressure on them, ask some basic questions:

"Where are you now with your business ? Where would you like to be ? What are you willing to do or change to get there ?" If you find out what they really want, you have permission to tell them what they need to do to get it. Remember you can't make anybody do anything, you can only suggest.

A great way to lose business associates is to push them to achieve goals for your gain. Good leaders always put their group's goals first. I watched people tell others in their group, "You should hit this volume, so I can get this bonus." That's the wrong motive and it isn't going to work. Help people hit THEIR GOALS and you will automatically hit yours. That's the right thing to do and the right thing to do for your long-term business.

A SIGN OF A GOOD LEADER: Do people bring their new people to you ? If your people are not bringing their new people to you, they don't trust you. You might want to fix that.

Passing information though your group is very important. To quote my friend and mentor Theron, "Make sure nobody's standing on the hose." Check down in your business from time to time to make sure the information is getting where it needs to go.

Let's talk about **Edification.** Your job is to edify your leaders and people who are doing what it takes to be leaders in their group, so their people will listen to them. This only works if your group edifies you to their group. Do not edify someone who is not active or is doing something different from what is taught in your organization.

Making things "easier" for people in your group is not always helpful. You can do too much for people and that can make them weak. Anyone who is always looking for an easy way will never perform at a high level. Don't do things for people they can do for themselves.

Some people always seem to find an exit. You never have to show it to them. Quitters will find an excuse to quit. All you can do is give them a reason to stay. That reason is usually hope. You as the leader are the hope-giver.

When building a People Business, it's all about following the leader's example. Would you want everyone in your business to duplicate you ?

LEADERSHIP ATTITUDE

**ATTITUDE
IS EVERYTHING !**

**ATTITUDE
IS EVERYTHING !**

Your ATTITUDE will be contagious in your group. A good attitude or bad. A cheerful positive person will attract people to them. A smile is worth a lot of money to you. Your attitude is always your choice. You will have mental downtime, just don't share it with your group. Never pass negative downline. A positive attitude may not solve all your problems but it will annoy enough of your negative relatives to make it worth the effort.

**WHEN ALL ELSE FAILS ...
THINK ABOUT THE MONEY !**

Try a Positive Attitude, I think you might like it.

DIFFERENCE BETWEEN A BOSS AND A LEADER

BOSS

Drives Employees
Depends on Authority
Inspires Fear
Says "I"
Places Blame for Mistakes
Uses People
Takes Credit
Commands
Says "Go"
Puts People Down

Coaches Associates
Depends on Goodwill
Generates Enthusiasm
Says "We"
Fixes Mistakes
Develops People
Gives Credit
Asks, Doesn't Command
Says "Let's Go"
Builds People Up

LEADER

ALWAYS REMEMBER
You're building a volunteer army. You are not the boss.
You are the leader of a group of INDEPENDENT associates.

A FEW MORE THOUGHTS

Don't try to make someone a leader that doesn't want to be a leader. Some people just want to be part of the team. Recognize them as great team players. Let them know how important they are to the team.

Don't talk effort with people, talk results. Talk about Their Goals and Their Dreams. Always take them back to their WHY.

Make sure the people you are working with know your success does not depend on them. You will be successful no matter what they do.

Always give credit to people. Recognize them at every level of achievement and performance.

Believe in people. That's all some folks need to be successful. They just need someone in their corner believing in them.

Foster enthusiasm. It's contagious. There are many types of enthusiasm. Give people the freedom to express it their way.

The only person you can rush is you. Let people move at their own speed.

Be confident. Know where you're going, even if you're lost.

Leadership is being an example to your group. Everything you do will be magnified 100 times. Your group will follow your example, GOOD or BAD.

Most of the information in this chapter was taken from my mentor's notes.
Thanks Theron

TWELVE

A PERSONALITY HUNT

SANGUINE   MELANCHOLIC   PHLEGMATIC   CHOLERIC

THE FOUR PERSONALITY TYPES

There are basically four types of personalities or temperaments you will deal with. It's very helpful as a leader to know the personality type of the person you're trying to counsel or help. How you teach or counsel them may be different depending on the personality type. There are really more than four types. Most people are a combination of two or more types. For example, I am perfectly balanced with all four types. At least that's what I tell my wife(she might not believe it). The good news is, whatever your type, you can build your business.

SANGUINE

They are very social, fun loving, outgoing, impulsive, persuasive, easily amused and distracted. They are great at building relationships. They fear rejection and want everybody to like them. They are very effective business builders if they can stay focused. If they were an animal, they would be an otter.

MELANCHOLIC

This is the engineer type or accountant. They can be introverted and thoughtful. Never late. Often perfectionists self-reliant and independent. Not easily swayed. Once they decide the business numbers work, they will do great. If they were an animal, it would be a beaver.

PHLEGMATIC

They are easy going, relaxed and quiet. Prefer stability over uncertainty, are consistent, calm, rational. Curious and observant. They are wonderful team players and want everybody to get along. If they were an animal, it would be a dog. Everybody's best friend.

CHOLERIC

They are ambitious, controllers, need to be in charge, can't understand why people don't do things their way. They get things done. They can be great leaders if they learn some people skills. Too often they fall into the "boss mode" and that won't work in a People Business. If they were an animal, it would be a lion.

WORKING WITH THE DIFFERENT PERSONALITY TYPES

SANGUINES

Working with the Sanguine, it's better to keep things simple and fun. Always keep their dream in front of them. They might not do well if their mentor is a strong Choleric unless their dream is big enough. They work better with an end goal instead of a step-by-step plan. Example: "The goal is to show your business plan three times a week." They will figure out their own steps to get the job done. Just keep praising them, they will do very well.

MELANCHOLIC

I always call this group "The Engineers" because that's how they think. They need a step-by-step organized plan. They will read the manual, unlike the sanguine who doesn't know there is a manual. Try to keep them from over thinking. Good luck. This is a true story: I have an associate in my business who was making his business presentation way too long and technical. I said, "Larry, you've got to simplify your plan." A couple days later we sat down and he showed me a three-page essay on "simple". That's how an engineer type thinks. I am always amazed how well this group does with building the People Business. A high percentage of the leaders in my business are Melancholic.

PHLEGMATIC
This type is the easiest to work with and teach. They will be great at following instructions and their group will love them. Just tell them what to do and let them know you will help them. Keep their dream in front of them.

CHOLERIC

This type is very goal oriented. Let them know what needs to be done to reach their goals and they will get it done. Keep an eye on the people they sponsor to make sure they are not being "bossed". This type can do great things and be great leaders.

ANY PERSONALITY TYPE CAN WIN THE GAME

There is no one personality type that is more successful than another. It's all about work ethic and learning some people skills. Each type has positive and negative traits when it comes to building a large People Business. The Choleric needs to chill out and not be a boss, but will be a great leader. The Melancholic needs to quit reading the manual and go do something, but will be very efficient. The Phlegmatic needs to quit worrying about if everyone in their group has a good bowel movement, but will treat their people great and their group will love them. The Sanguine has to quit throwing keggers and act like a business person, but will have a fun, growing business because everyone will want to be with them. Everybody can win !

I noticed most of the successful people have spouses that will be opposite of their personality. The sanguine may have a melancholic spouse. This is a very good thing because they will balance each other. You don't want two cholerics in the house; that's like putting two cats in a bag. If you have two sanguines nothing may get done, but it will be a great party.

No matter the personality type, you have the ability to do great things with your business. Understanding how others think and how they work will be very helpful in building your People Business.

Tip: Knowing how different personalities think can also be helpful
with understanding friends and family members.

Great books to read
YOUR PERSONALITY TREE
by Florence Littauer

THE FIVE LOVE LANGUAGES
by Gary Chapman
(Marriage book)

PEOPLE WILL DO MORE FOR A BBQ

I'm always amazed how you can show someone how to be financially free by just doing a few simple things consistently in their business and they always find something to distract them from what they need to do. But if I say "Show your business plan three times a week for a month and you can come to a cookout," they will show the plan three times a week. People always do more for a barbeque than they will for their financial future. I guess it's all about a short term goal they can see and not being left out of the party.

This is a good thing to know. I learned it early in my business. Don't be afraid to have fun building your business. Being part sanguine, (remember I'm perfectly balanced in all four personalities) I loved putting together "events". Be sure to check with your mentors before you do anything for the first time. You don't want to hurt your business. We would sometimes put a qualification of either volume or activity on being able to attend the event but other times we just got people together.

Here are a few things we did with our group. Remember check with your mentors first. We had a family picnic in the park every year with games and contests for adults and kids. We rented a theatre and showed reward trips and group events from the year before and had leaders speak. We had car rallies, volleyball tournaments and laser tag. We even had a cardboard boat building contest and raced the boats in a lake (don't try this at home).Use your imagination. The events can be a great way to unify your group and help people do things they should be doing anyway. Have some fun with your business ! (Somebody might have to explain to the melancholics what fun is.)

GOAL SETTING & BABY STEPS

HAPPINESS IS THE PROGRESSIVE REALIZATION OF WORTHWHILE DREAMS AND GOALS

I can't over stress the importance of goal setting. You must have a target to shoot at. If you have the attitude of "I will get there when I get there". You probably won't get there. Take the time to figure out what you want, when you want it and what you're willing to do to get it. Don't be afraid to let yourself dream big. Lots of people "wish" for things in their lives. I hear them say, "I wish I had more family time". "I wish I could afford a nicer home". A wish is just saying, "I don't like the way things are" but a DREAM says "I want to achieve something". A goal with a plan makes it all real.

"Whatever the mind can conceive and believe it can achieve"

Napoleon Hill

Think about your perfect life. Are you living it now or are you just getting by ? Do you have a plan or direction ? Goal setting will let you set a direction for your life's goals and dreams. It's kind of a big deal !

People who write down their goals are 42% more likely to achieve their goals than people who do not write them down. Telling someone and speaking your goals increases achievement to 78%. When you write and speak your goals your subconscious mind begins to work on bringing things together to make things happen. You will start to run into people and situations that will move you closer to your goals.

A DREAM WRITTEN DOWN WITH A DATE BECOMES A GOAL
A GOAL BROKEN DOWN INTO STEPS BECOMES A PLAN

A PLAN BACKED BY ACTION MAKES DREAMS COME TRUE

Making a game plan to fulfill your goals is a must. The best way to do that is to sit down with your mentor and draw out a plan. Where, when and how to work your business to get where you need to go. You are probably very busy and may have a family. You need to work all this into your plan.

Here is an example of a game plan my mentor drew out for me.
We mapped out how I could expose my business plan 8 times a week.

MON	TUES	WED	THURS	FRI	SAT	SUN	
WORK					F A M	F A M I L Y	NON BIZ HOURS
STP	STP	STP	STP	STP			BIZ HOURS
F A M	S T P	F A M	S T P	F A M	S T P		**STP MEANS SHOW THE PLAN** Expose Your Business

Map out your business plan and business hours.

S.M.A.R.T. GOALS

S.   **SPECIFIC:** State exactly what you want to achieve. The WHO, WHAT, WHEN, WHERE and WHY. A specific goal has a better chance of being accomplished than a general goal.

M.   **MEASURABLE:** Track your progress. Know what you need to do to move forward to meet your end goal. Short term goals will keep you motivated.

A.   **ATTAINABLE:** Goals should push you a little out of your comfort zone but still be in your reach and achievable. A goal you have control over.

R.   **REALISTIC:** Is your goal realistic ? Be careful with this one. Your relatives and friends "realistic" might be different than yours. Ask your mentors what they think.

T.   **TIMELY:** Set a time frame for your goal. Actual date. This is important to keep you moving. Tell someone your time goal. This will keep you accountable.

Tip: Never change your goal, just change the date.
Set a new date and keep moving.

BABY STEPS

Take everything one step at a time. Don't get overwhelmed. Remember the old joke, "How do you eat an elephant ? … One bite at a time". Think long-term. Focus on what you need to do today. Take care of today and tomorrow will take care of itself.

Too many people overestimate what they can accomplish short-term and underestimate what they can accomplish long-term. You can get frustrated by not growing as fast as you would like. Just stay steady and you will accomplish your goals. I remember hearing an audio that said "If you're going to fall, fall forward". You will fall, that's part of the game of success. Pick yourself up, dust yourself off and keep moving forward. There will be times when your business grows fast and other times, not so much. Enjoy the ride. Always keep your eyes on the prize.

Everyone has fears and issues they need to overcome to build their People Business. It's usually one or two things that keep us from our success. Identify those things and use the "baby step" principle to conquer them. For example: If you have a hard time talking to strangers, don't go out and try to talk to everybody and use fancy scripts. Just go out and say "Hi" to someone. Start small. Do that every day and soon you will be comfortable. Then say "Hi, how's your day going?" Baby steps. Break everything into small bites and keep eating.

YOU WILL HIT YOUR GOALS !
I'm not sure what an elephant tastes like but I know you will love
the taste of FREEDOM !

BABY STEPPING TO YOUR GOALS

FiFTEEN

THROWING LIFE RINGS

Picture yourself in a life raft in the middle of the ocean and all around you are people treading water waiting to be rescued. Your only job is to throw life rings to those people and if they grab the ring, you pull them into the boat. You do not want to jump in the water because they will pull you under. Just throw the rings. Here's what will happen in your business. You'll throw the life ring to someone and they'll say, "No thanks, I really like it out here." or "I'm too busy right now to grab anything." Here's the one I like. "I knew a guy one time who got into one of those life raft things and it sunk. You're not going to fool me". You just keep throwing the life rings and finally someone grabs the ring and holds on tight. You pull them into the boat and they say, "THANKS FOR SAVING MY LIFE". That's what it's all about. It's not how many rings you throw, it's how many people you save. It's your job to throw, it's their job to grab the ring. Someone threw you a life ring. Now it's your turn.

You are going to do great things with your People Business. You were not made to be average. You were made for greatness ! You will inspire others to be great. You have an awesome future ahead of you.

Get the "**BUTS**" out of your life. "I want to meet people, **BUT** I'm shy". "I want to build a big business **BUT**, I don't know a lot of people". "I want security for my family **BUT**, I'm afraid". Well Cowboy Up Buttercup, it's time to ride. This is your time. This is your life. Grab it and hang on. Grab onto your mentor's teaching. Hold on to your belief in what you're trying to accomplish and never let go of your DREAMS !

This is going to be a fun ride to financial freedom and a lifestyle you can only imagine. Now be thankful you are not normal. "Normal" people never do great things.

Now go throw those Life Rings !

OTHER BOOKS THAT COULD
HELP YOU OUT

The Dream Giver (Spiritual) * Bruce Wilkinson

The Legend of the Monk& the Merchant (Spiritual) * Terry Felber

Sequoia Sized Success (Spiritual) * Paul Tsika

What You Seed is What You Get (Spiritual) * Paul Tsika

The Generosity Factor * Ken Blanchard & S.Truett Cathy

Fields to Freedom * Frank Morales

A Better Way to Live * Og Mandino

The Go Getter * Peter B. Kyne

How To Be Rich * J. Paul Getty

Acres Of Diamonds * Russel H. Conwell

Richest Man in Babylon * George S. Clason

The Choice * Og Mandino

Greatest Salesman (Spiritual) * Og Mandino

The Tongue-A Creative Force (Spiritual) * Charles Capps

God Wants You to Be Rich (Spiritual) * Paul Zane Pilzer

More Than Enough * Dave Ramsey

I Will Teach You To Be Rich * Ramit Sethi

GOALS & DREAMS
(Write them down)
WISH, WANT, NEED, GOT.
Everyone wishes, everyone wants but until it gets to a NEED,
nothing will happen.

How much money do you want to make annually in your business ?

$ _____

What is your time frame for accomplishing this ? _____

How many hours a week will you put in your business ? _____

What is your time frame for replacing your job income ? _____
(If that is your goal)

Where & What kind of home(s) do you want ?

Where ? _____ How big ? _____

What kind of car(s) do you want to own ? _____

Where do you want to travel ?

What charities do you want to support ?

Are you plugged into a mentor ?

NOTES

Don't mess with my
Business
Or my Mind.

My wife Doesn't understand my
Business !

Make New Business Friends
Online

First Prospect
Call

If you're not having fun, you're doing it wrong !

gsgilmour@gmail.com

www.ingramcontent.com/pod-product-compliance
Lightning Source LLC
Chambersburg PA
CBHW082303200526
45168CB00017B/2755